100+ Fun Ideas for

Practising Primary Languages through Drama and Performance

Janet Lloyd

We hope you and your pupils enjoy using the ideas in this book. Listed below are a few of our other books which might be of interest to you. Information on these and all our other books can be found on our website: www.brilliantpublications.co.uk.

100+ Fun Ideas for Practising MFL in the Primary Classroom
More Fun Ideas for Advancing MFL in the Primary Classroom
Physical French Phonics
Learn French with Luc et Sophie
J'aime Beaucoup Chanter en Français
Chantez Plus Fort
Singt mit uns
Vamos a Cantar

Published by Brilliant Publications
Unit 10
Sparrow Hall Farm
Edlesborough
Dunstable
Bedfordshire
LU6 2ES, UK

www.brilliantpublications.co.uk

The name Brilliant Publications and the logo are registered trademarks.

Written by Janet Lloyd
Illustrations and cover illustration by Emily Skinner

ISBN 978-1-78317-121-7
ebook 978–1-78317-122-4

First printed and published in the UK in 2014

Contents

Drama games – listening, speaking, reading, writing

Making a drama out of story and culture!

Explorations of art and music

Sketches

Foreword

The purpose of this book is to offer teachers a wide range of activities to practice listening, speaking, reading and writing in the target language with young learners who are beginners, moving on or advanced primary language learners. The book has suggestions for activities that can reinforce grammar and the structure of language through physical performance and creativity.

The activities are divided into four sections:

- ✦ Drama games – a range of games that explore listening to the target language, listening and speaking in the target language, and listening, speaking, reading and writing in the language.
- ✦ Making a drama out of story and culture – target language creative performances and character exploration based upon story and culture.
- ✦ Explorations of art and music – using the medium of art or music to develop target language simple spoken dialogues and descriptions, poems, raps and creative physical performances.
- ✦ Sketches – bringing together listening, speaking, reading and writing to create simple sketches and more challenging creative spoken performances.

Watch out for the GRAMMAR ALERTS! as these are activities where the children and you can explore simple grammar and sentence structure.

The activities are coded to show their suitability for learners at different stages:

- ✦ Beginners (up to one year of language learning)
- ✦ Moving on (two to three years of language learning progression)
- ✦ Advanced (three to four years of language learning progression)

Drama games – listening and responding

The drama and performance activities here help children appreciate and internalise the sound patterns, intonation, cadence and phonics of the target language. The children are involved in observing and reinterpreting sound and sound patterns of words, sentences and short texts.

1. Single word or phrase mimes

Level: beginners

✦ Use single word or phrase mimes for target language learning beginners. Ask pupils to mime the words or phrases a teacher or partner says.

2. Short text message mimes

Level: moving on

✦ Listen to a text – a song, a poem or questions and answers in a dialogue – and ask the children to convey the meaning of the text in a mime. (The sequence of mimes conveys the message of the text in this case.)

3. A group mime

Level: advanced

- Each child is responsible for a part of a longer listening text.
- The teacher plays the class a longer message, eg a song with four or five verses or a conversation made up of six questions and answers.
- The children are put into groups depending on how the teacher divides up the text. Each child in the group is given a number (not in the same order as the parts of text).
- The teacher calls out a number and the children with that number go to the teacher and listen again to their part of the text. Each child must put together a mime of what they have heard the teacher say and convey the message to their group.
- The children perform their mimes to their groups in random order and then the group must reconstruct their mime message as a series of mime performances in what they think is the correct order.
- The whole class listens to the whole text again. Do the groups want to change the order of their mimes?

4. Rhythm identikits

Level: all

✦ This activity can be used with single words, short utterances or longer texts. It can help the children to internalise and remember the language you are practising and focus on the intonation and tone of the language.

✦ Can the class help you to identify the rhythm in a short utterance, a sentence or a series of questions and answers? Can the class clap out the rhythm with you?

✦ Now try calling out a phrase and ask the children to respond just with the rhythm.

✦ Beat out a rhythm – can the class say the phrase in words?

5. Rhythm reports

Level: all

✦ Can the children help you to make a rhythm report of a text? This means that they listen with you to a text and create the rhythm by tapping / clapping or beating out the message without saying any words.

✦ They must then perform the rhythm alongside the spoken text said by you or played on a sound file.

6. A class rhythm performance

Level: all

- Use percussion instruments to make text into a performance. You need to create 'rhythm reports' (activity 5) first.
- Once you have a 'rhythm report' then divide the class into two parts – with half the class creating the rhythm and the other half of the class performing the text as one communal voice.

7. Passing on the beat

Level: beginners and moving on

- Beginners: working in pairs, the children challenge each other to pass on the beat. One partner listens to a short message from the other partner in the target language and performs it as a 'beat without words message'. Does it sound like the message with words? Does it pass on the beat? They then swap roles.
- Moving on: Play a couple of games in pairs of the simple pass on the beat game above. Now ask the children to listen to a series of sentences in the target language and in pairs to create the beat of the sentences. Can one pair challenge a second pair to spot their 'pass on the beat' sentence from the series of spoken sentence-length utterances?

8. Sound signals

Level: beginners

✦ The class must decide upon actions (sound signals) which convey types of sounds we might hear in key target language words.

Is it an explosive sound?

Is it a sharp sound?

Is it a long slow sound?

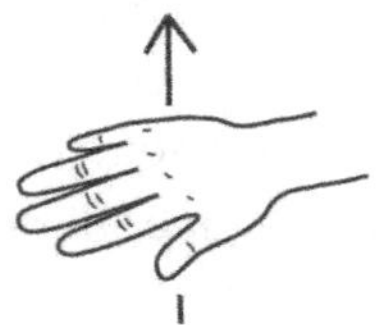

Is it a forced sound?

✦ Now share words with the children: adjectives, nouns or verbs. Can the children listen to the sounds in the words and convey the strongest sound in the word as a sound signal?

✦ Can one child challenge another to identify the word that they have conveyed as a sound signal?

9. Sound and meaning interpreters

Level: moving on and advanced

✦ This is a physical activity so children need some space for this to work well – hall or playground would work well. The children listen to a text – song, rhyme, poem, story – and then have to convey this through movement and interpretation of sound. They should work with a partner; one partner conveys the meaning of the text through mime and the second partner conveys the sound of the words and phrases.

✦ A warm up to this activity would be to practise the 'sound signals' activities above. Make the sentence/text into a string of sounds as in the sound signal activity. (You may end up with an explosive sound and a soft sound in a word followed by a fast sound and a short high sound in the next word etc.)

10. Visualisation

Level: moving on and advanced

✦ This activity is similar to the above activity. Ask the children to find a safe space in the hall and ask them to listen to a familiar song, poem or story in the target language. Ask them to take part in what they hear and to convey the story through movement.

✦ If you are certain that all children will be safe, ask them to close their eyes and perform the story as they hear it.

✦ Ask for volunteers to share their own performance and visualisation with the class. Ask the children to share with you afterwards how the performances that they have watched differ?

11. Sound waves 1

Level: beginners (with short utterances) moving on (sentence level) and advanced (series of sentences in a short text)

✦ This is a listening and responding activity based upon frequency pictures that we see on a computer screen when we record our voices.

✦ Let the children watch the frequency picture of a spoken sentence or text in the target language. Ask the children to think about why the waves change shape and what this tells us about the sound that is being amplified. How might we convey physical performance sound waves? Ask the children to stand up and watch the frequency waves on a screen while you play some sound files.

✦ Play the sentence or text again. Can the children create physical movements using their entire body which correspond to the frequency picture they can see?

✦ Share several listening texts with frequency pictures with the children. Ask them to explore the sound wave picture they would make for each of the texts.

✦ Play a game where the class need to guess the target language that a child is conveying through his/her sound wave performance.

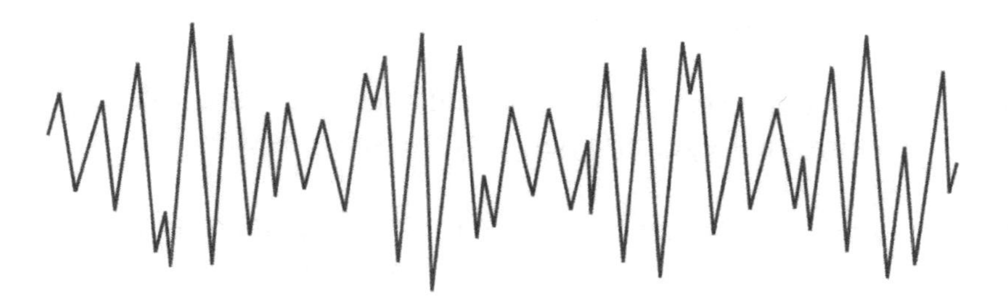

Drama games – speaking and listening

The drama and performance activities here help children to develop their ability to listen accurately and to mimic sound patterns, intonation, cadence and phonics of the target language in the spoken word. The children are involved in observing and reinterpreting sound and sound patterns of words, sentences and short texts and in creating simple spoken performances linked with movement and actions.

12. Freeze frames

Level: all

- This is a simple technique that can be used to make certain that children are participating in a spoken text accurately or as an AfL (assessment for learning) opportunity.
- For beginners, pause the counting of a sequence of numbers between 0 and 10 and ask the children to hold up the number of fingers that represent the next number. You can ask the children also to repeat objects after you in different voices and then call a halt and ask the children to try to physically create the shape of an object or make a facial gesture or emotion they associate with a particular colour.
- With learners who are moving on you can use communal spoken language activities, such as a familiar song, rhyme or poem. Freeze frame the children by pausing the song or halting the class and asking them to strike the pose of the last word or phrase.

- For example, if the last word was 'cat' then they must take the pose of a cat or, if it was a weather phrase, they have to freeze frame as snow or rain, etc.

- For advanced learners, set up transactional role plays where children, in pairs, generate dialogues and conversations. Ask the children to perform the dialogues from memory. Freeze frame the class during the dialogues. Ask the children to freeze in character.

- Bring one pair to life and hold a class 'listen in' while this pair now performs some of their dialogue.

- Now ask the children to work with a new partner and hold a similar conversation. When you think the children are ready to perform, hold another freeze frame 'listen in' activity with these new partnerships and dialogues.

13. Tableau

Level: all

- A tableau is a technique in drama to gather quite a large group of people together in a scene or setting. In the first instance a group of people come together silently and in character. In language learning we could ask children working in groups of 6 or 8 to come together for a picnic or a birthday party as a group of friends or as a family.

- Using thought tracking and teacher modelling, can the children decide what their characters might say in the scene, based upon the language the class has been practising, for example, asking for food, wishing people a happy birthday, saying thank you for a present etc. Encourage children to think about what the person they are pretending to be might say or think.

- Now the children can bring their tableau to life and find a second person to say their phrases to, keeping in the character of the person they have decided to be at the party or picnic.

14. Speak and perform dominoes

Level: all

- ✦ At beginners level, say (or play a sound file of) a sequence of words from a common theme, eg colours, numbers, animals, foods, days, months.

- ✦ Can the children create a domino effect performance of the words with an action? Each word must link to the next word, eg colours in the order of the rainbow, numbers in a sequence. Each action should be interconnected so it leads into the next action. For example if you are making a 'speak and perform dominoes' sequence of the days of the week then you would need an end movement for Monday's action (eg going to school) which leads into the beginning movement for Tuesday's action (eg going swimming).

- ✦ These performances can be one child after another, each performing one of the words, or all the children performing all the words together. The words and the actions should flow.

- ✦ At moving on and advanced level this could be a sequence of sentences introducing someone or describing something or a series of questions and answers.

15. Eavesdropping

Level: all

- The children work with a partner. One is designated Partner A and the other Partner B.
- The teacher calls all Partner As to come and listen to a phrase. They must then go back to their partner and repeat to Partner B what they have heard, with the same actions, type of voice and volume. The Partner Bs must then practise what they see and hear.
- When the teacher calls for all the Partner Bs, they must go to the teacher and share what they have heard with the rest of the Partner B children, trying to replicate the same actions, voice and volume they have observed from Partner A.
- Swap roles and repeat.

16. Listen, rewind and perform

Level: all

- You need a large space to organise the class into four groups with some distance between the groups. The hall would be a good place to try this activity using the corners as bases for the groups.

- Give each group a name. The teacher gives each group a familiar phrase, sentence or a series of sentences. The groups need to decide on actions, voice, volume and performance of their specific message. Give the groups time to work on their performance.

- The teacher then asks each group in turn to perform their message for another group. The second group have an allotted amount of time to rewind the performance by discussing what they heard and saw. They can ask for a replay should they need this.

- Then they must try to re-perform the message performance exactly as they heard and saw it. The first group now perform their message a second time – how near to perfect was the second group's rewind performance?

- Repeat this activity so that each group can perform, and then rewind and perform another group's message.

- With more advanced learners, the message could become a dialogue of questions and answers where each group's message is part of the whole message. Children must discuss and determine the sensible order of the sub-messages to create a final order for the whole class message. Can the class put the dialogue as a spoken dialogue together and create a rewind performance of all the messages?

17. Rewind: play it again Sam!

Level: moving on and advanced (although you may feel with a familiar rhyme or song beginner learners could develop a similar activity)

✦ In this activity one child observes a second child's spoken performance of a rhyme or poem or a simple description (eg some sentences to describe oneself, a description of an animal's colour and size, a short list of instructions to make or do something, a list of months and birthdays, etc). The performer needs to add a suitable voice, volume and a performance element, perhaps using one or two props.

✦ The observer must watch and listen carefully and then rewind the performance and, as it says in the title, 'play it again Sam' by delivering the same performance.

18. Robots

Level: all

GRAMMAR ALERT! Commands

✦ With beginners concentrate on short instructional text, eg commands; with learners who are moving on, focus on several sentences using instructional text and directions. With advanced learners use several sentences with a mixture of instructional text and directions, adverbs and prepositions.

✦ Children work with a partner and give the partner instructions that they must follow. One partner speaks (as if programming a robot) and the other partner listens and responds and carries out the activity in a robotic manner.

19. Emotion voice overs

Level: all

- Children work in pairs. One child says some familiar statements with no emotion at all. The second child should repeat the statement, adding emotion and a style of voice to bring the spoken statement to life.
- The children could record both versions of their statements.
- Play these sound recordings back to the class; pause after the flat statement and ask the children to discuss, with a talking partner, ways of saying the statement with emotion.
- Now play the second recording of the statement with the emotion voice over. Who came up with similar ideas and who came up with different ideas for the performance?

20. Emoticons

Level: moving on, advanced

- This is a simple observation game which works well with emotions and feelings.
- Ask children to volunteer to come out to the front. Whisper a phrase or word that conveys an emotion to the child (eg I am tired/ I am hungry/ I am happy). They must say and perform the phrase for the class, but they can decide to convey a different emotion to the one they say.
- Can the class decide if it's true or false – does the phrase match the action?

21. Question and answer chant challenge

Level: beginners

- ✦ You will need a large space for this activity. Divide the class into two groups. Stand them opposite each other and at a distance from each other. One line is in charge of questions and one line is in charge of answers. Designate a captain for each team.

- ✦ The object of the game is for the lines to move progressively closer to each other, getting less and less loud and aggressive in their actions as the lines converge.

- ✦ The captain of the question team chooses a team member to lead the team's question. That person says the question in a certain voice, with certain actions, and the rest of the team copy this person. The answers team now thinks of its response and the captain chooses someone to lead the response and all the team performs it. Each team moves one step nearer the other line after each question and answer. As they get closer their voices and actions should get smaller, quieter and less threatening.

- ✦ Swap the roles of the teams and play the chant challenge again.

Drama games – speaking

The drama games here are based on speaking activities that can be accessed by different learners at different stages of their acquisition of the target language. The activities encourage the learners to focus on pronunciation, intonation, memory and recall and enable the learners to grow in confidence in their ability to use the spoken language.

22. Object machines

Level: beginners

GRAMMAR ALERT! Commands

✦ This is a very simple speaking activity. Give each child a familiar noun, adjective or verb. They have 60 seconds to create a shape or form with their bodies that portrays the word eg a big sunshine shape for the adjective yellow or a cat-like figure to portray the word cat. Their bodies are now working as 'object machines' which must produce an item that looks and sounds like the object or something closely associated with the object.

23. Number machines

Level: beginners

✦ Ask children in groups of three to create number machines, using numbers the class knows (eg 0-20). The machine must have the correct pronunciation of the words, portray the type of shape and sound of the word (eg a 'round' shape and sound etc) through physical movements.

✦ Each child performs one number and the group's numbers must connect together, so one child's number performance physically connects by hand/arm etc to the next number and triggers the next child's performance.

✦ The group could decide to just use even numbers or prime numbers or numbers in reverse. During the performances can the class spot the type of number sequence they are trying to convey?

24. Insta-drams

Level: all

✦ This is a quick and easy way to re-cap personal information. Show the class a picture of a scene in which two people are talking with each other. What do the children think the people are saying? The children have two minutes in pairs to come up with the phrases they think the characters are saying. Ask three or four children to share what they think the question and answer in the picture might be. Agree as a class which fits best.

✦ Now ask the children, working in pairs, to make the chosen question and answer into an 'insta – dram'. They must perform with their partner the question and answer with feelings and actions.

✦ Show a second picture and create the next insta-dram.

25. Selfie speaking photograph

Level: all

✦ Ask the children to think of everything that they can say about themselves in the target language so far. Ask them to take a pose (as if they are about to take a selfie photograph). They should stay in that pose whilst they say everything they can about themselves. The pose must be linked to their personality or what they are telling the audience. Only their mouths must move as they speak and create their 'selfie' speaking photograph.

26. Flowing sentences

Level: moving on or advanced

✦ Give children (in groups of 5) five different idea prompts, eg if they are describing an animal:

- One child must name the type of animal
- One child must say its colour
- One child must say its size
- One child must give it a name, etc.

✦ The children must individually create their own spoken sentence. The children must then work as a group to put the sentences together to create a sequence of flowing sentences that convey the character of the object, whether this is a ferocious lion or (if the class are focusing on family) a kind and gentle grandma etc.

27. Concertina characters

Level: advanced

- ✦ Ask the children to think of all the ways they can describe themselves – their physical description, their emotions, their characteristics, personal information.

- ✦ Now they must use their bodies to create a verbal portrait of themselves. The children must explore their own personal space and evolve into the full person they are – starting off as a statue or as a small tight ball and growing into themselves with each phrase they say. Each action must reflect the message they are trying to convey in each sentence they utter.

28. Syllable squeeze

Level: beginners

- ✦ Stand two children face to face. One child says a sound from one of the familiar words you have been practising, emphasising the sound with facial movement. The second child must guess the whole word and say it, making sure that the syllable the first child said is performed exactly as the first child performed it. Swap roles.

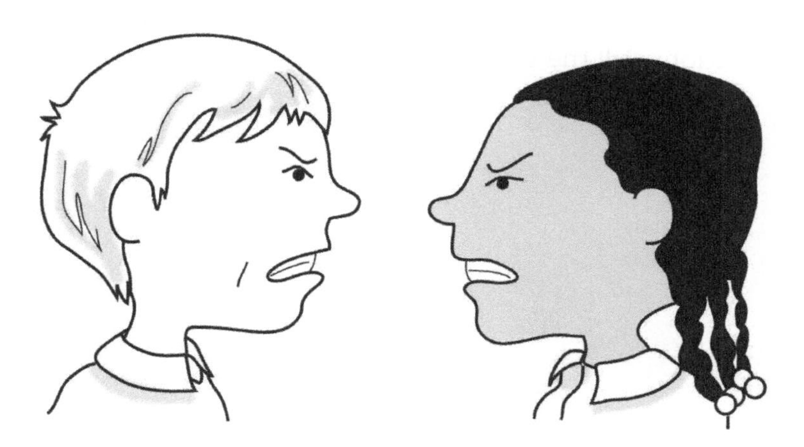

29. Raps

Level: all

- Take a simple sequence of sentences, a rhyme or verse from a song and ask the children to add rhythm, beat and performance to create a rap they can perform for the class. Film the raps and play them again.

- Alternatively, use an App such as www.smule.com to create a rap to play again for the class.

30. Follow my leader actions and utterances

Level: beginners and moving on

- Sit the children in a circle and say a phrase with an action. It should pass around the group exactly as you said and performed it.

- Now whisper a phrase (as in Chinese whispers) to a child with clear actions. The children must whisper the message to each other and, at the same time, clearly perform the actions that go with the message. Does the phrase come out the same at the end when the last person speaks it? Are the actions still the same?

31. Follow my leader actions and silent utterances

Level: all

- ✦ Pass a silent phrase around the group. This works best if you ask for two volunteers to be the first and last child.
- ✦ The first child has to listen and then act out what they hear. The last child needs to feel confident that they will be able to observe and interpret the actions they see being passed around the group and be able to think of and say an appropriate target language phrase.
- ✦ The teacher whispers a phrase to the first child. This child must not speak but must act out the phrase for the next child. Each child passes just the actions on around the circle. The final child should do the actions and say the phrase they think has been passed around the group. Is it the correct phrase?

32. Back to back Q and A

Level: all

✦ Stand two children back to back. One child can only ask questions and the other child can only give answers. They must decide upon their questions and answers before they get in to position. They need to stand very still and not use facial gesture, only their arms and hands to convey the emotion of the questions and answers. The children need time to work this through individually and decide whether arm actions are slow and meaningful or rapid and full of excitement etc. This will depend on the question and also the response. For example:

Possible question/answer	Possible movement
How are you feeling?	as this is a caring question, gentle open movement of both arms
I am tired	hand/arm over mouth to indicate yawning

✦ The first performance of the questions and answers is back to back. Now turn the children to face each other and ask them to deliver the same performance of the questions and answers.

✦ Finally ask the children to perform the whole dialogue and actions again this time adding facial gestures.

✦ Discuss with the children how the dialogue changed as they moved from back to back, to facing each other without facial gestures, to adding facial gestures. Did the dialogue become more meaningful? Why?

33. Physical pop-ups

Level: beginners

- You need space for this activity.
- Give children several words from a sequence you have been practising and ask them to move from one side of the hall to the other generating physical pop-ups as they go!
- A physical pop-up is made up of the word, a volume and type of voice associated with the word and a large physical movement which conveys the meaning of the word. Each movement must flow into the next movement. For example, can they cross the hall using physical pop-ups for numbers 0–10, for colours, for weather phrases?
- Ask for volunteers to perform their physical pop-ups.

34. Hot seating

Level: advanced

- Brainstorm with the children all the personal information questions and answers they have practised (name, age, where he/she lives, likes, dislikes, character, feelings, sports, hobbies, favourite subject and foods, etc). Give a volunteer a picture of an imaginary or familiar character. (In this instance it's easiest if the character is imaginary because the volunteer has a free choice of responses.)
- Can the volunteer stand the hot seat for one minute, two minutes, three…? The volunteer must be in character in the way he/she responds – voice, actions, manner. Put on a countdown timer and start the questioning from the class.

35. On the hunt (Je cherche ... qui...)

Level: all (beginners will have a more limited amount of questions and answers to use)

✦ Send a volunteer out of the room. Whilst the volunteer is out of the classroom, decide upon the emotion with the class, eg happy, sad, tired, bored, silly, funny, sporty, etc. Select a child to answer in that way. This is the only child who will respond in this way. Everyone else can select a different manner and voice for their response. Now call the volunteer back into the room.

The volunteer must find a person who responds to his or her question with a voice and manner that matches an emotion the teacher will say in the target language. Ask the volunteer 'Find me the person who is...' (add the emotion you have decided upon). The volunteer can only ask five children. Can they find the responder amongst these five questions?

36. Sound waves 2

Level: beginners (with short utterances), moving on learners (with sentences), advanced (with a series of sentences in a short text)

- ✦ This activity extends activity 11: Sound waves 1 to include speaking too.
- ✦ Let the children watch the frequency picture of a spoken sentence or text in the target language from a sound file on a screen. Ask the children to think about why the waves change shape and what this tells us about the sound that is being amplified. How might we convey physical and spoken performance sound waves?
- ✦ Ask the children to stand up and watch the screen whilst you play some listening texts and display the frequency waves generated.
- ✦ Play the sentence or text again. Can the children add movement by responding to the frequency picture they can see? Can they now mimic the spoken word and add this to their performance?
- ✦ Increase the length and speed of the listening text for more advanced learners.
- ✦ Now give the learners a text, without displaying the frequency waves. Can the children create performances of spoken text from the listening file that include physical performances of the possible frequency waves too?
- ✦ Share performances with the class.

37. Dynamic four-way conversations

Level: moving on and advanced

✦ You will need to play some mime, listen and respond and also listen, respond and speak games first to practise 'conversation continuity phrases' such as:

- And you?
- Me too!
- I agree
- Really?
- That's good
- What a shame!

Explain to the children that these are the phrases that will turn a dialogue into a conversation.

✦ Ask the children, in pairs, to create a simple dialogue based upon language you have already practised with the children. An ideal scenario would be talking about how they are feeling and giving a reason why, saying what they are doing today (eg playing a sport/ listening to music/ watching a film) and giving an opinion. The children will need to practise their dialogues so they are secure with their questions and answers. Ask them also to think of ways to greet other people and practise ways to ask other people the same question using 'conversation continuity phrases'.

✦ Now match each pair with another pair in the class. Can they make their dialogues grow into a conversation? They must first of all watch and listen to each others' dialogues. Then they must try to run the dialogues into each other – finding spaces and points where the questions and answers from each dialogue can fit. They will need to add appropriate conversation continuity phrases to do this.

- When the children have created conversations out of dialogues where all four children are participating, can they add conversation dynamics – actions, gesture, facial expression and nonverbal emotions such as laughter or sighs?

- Film the children's conversations and create a visual gallery of the class' dynamic conversations.

38. Mirror game in the style of...

Level: moving on and advanced

- In this activity the children work with a partner. Discuss first what a mirror reflection shows and what they need to do to show the mirror image of their partner. For example, if the person looking in the mirror lifts their left hand, the person in the mirror needs to lift their right hand, both exactly at the same time.

- The challenge here is for the child who has the role of the person in the mirror to say a phrase exactly like their partner says it. They need to use the same facial gestures, same mouth movements, at the same time. They need to practise each mirrored phrase at least five times before they move on to another phrase.

- Hold 'listen and watch ins' after each phrase has been practised – where the class watch a mirror mime and give positive critical feedback on how synchronised the mime is and what can be done to make it even better.

39. Mirror game directions

Level: moving on and advanced

GRAMMAR ALERT! Commands

- ✦ In this activity the children work with a partner. As with activity 38, begin with a discussion of how a mirror works.
- ✦ The challenge here for the child in the mirror is to follow exactly the directions given so that he/she moves a designated part of the body, eg left arm up, right arm down, left leg forwards, right leg backwards. The aim of the child who speaks is to create a clear spoken description and also physical movements or shapes that both the person in the mirror and him/herself can create, as a sequence of synchronised movements.
- ✦ Hold 'listen and watch ins' after each phrase has been practised. The class watch a mirror mime and give positive critical feedback on how synchronised the mime is and what can be done to make it even better

40. Mirror game movements

Level: moving on and advanced

GRAMMAR ALERT! Commands, adverbs

✦ In this activity the children work with a partner. As with activity 38, begin with a discussion of how a mirror works.

✦ The challenge here is to work on directions, commands and adverbs, eg quickly, slowly, etc. The child in the mirror must synchronise their moves exactly with the child who says and controls the movement, the direction and possibly the speed of the action eg 'lift your right hand slowly'.

✦ Hold 'listen and watch ins' after each phrase has been practised – where the class watch a mirror mime and give positive critical feedback on how synchronised the mime is and what can be done to make it even better.

41. Flowing items – pass it on

Level: all

✦ This is a game of physical 'Pass the parcel'. It's great for practising new language, eg animals, weather, clothes etc. Stand the children in a circle. Show an item and ask the first child to your left to name the item and add an action. Now can the children pass the word and the action around the circle, as seamlessly as possible. Whatever the first child did the rest of the circle should copy.

✦ Divide the large circle into smaller circles of 10 children and set up similar activities with picture prompts for each circle. Hold 'watch and listen ins' to see how the different groups have approached the same language items in the picture prompts.

42. Flowing phrases – pass it on and add something

Level: moving on

- This activity extends activity 41 by adding adjectives.

- Model for the class with a group of six children. Stand the children in a circle. Show an item and ask the child to your left to name the item and add an action. The second child must copy the action, say the word in the same style as the first child and add a colour with another action. The third child performs what he/she has seen and heard and adds another colour and action. Now can the children in the circle pass the word and the action on as seamlessly as possible? Whatever action the first child did, the rest of the circle should copy.

- Divide your class into circles of six children and set up similar activities with picture prompts for each circle. Hold 'watch and listen ins' to see how the different groups have approached the same language items in the picture prompts.

43. Flowing sentences – pass it on, add something and share

Level: advanced

GRAMMAR ALERT! Creating simple sentences with verbs

✦ This activity builds on activity 42 by adding verbs in the first person singular that the class have already learned (eg I see, I eat, I like) and adverbs.

✦ Model for the class with a group of six children. Stand the children in a circle. Show an item and ask the first child to your left to name the item and select a verb that fits with the item. The first child says the phrase with actions for the verb and adds an action for the item. The second child must copy the actions, say the phrase in the style the first child said it and add a colour and an adverb (with actions). The third child performs what he/she has seen and heard and adds an additional adjective (and action). The fourth child adds a second adverb (and action) and finally the fifth child must be prepared to share the sentence they have created with the class. The fifth child now becomes the first child and the activity begins again.

Drama games – listening, speaking, reading, writing

These drama and performance activities help children to develop their ability to use the target language accurately in all four skills. They help the children to develop their creative use of language and to explore the structure of the language through physical activities. The children continue to explore how to copy sound patterns accurately, develop intonation, cadence and phonics of the target language in the spoken word and read the written word accurately. The children are involved in observing and reinterpreting spoken and written patterns of words, sentences and short texts and in creating simple spoken performances linked with movement and actions.

44. Charades with a written twist

Level: all

✦ This simple and well-known party game works really well in the language learning classroom! One child silently reads an item, phrase or sentences from a card and then mimes this for the class. Can the class guess the mime? The class can write down on their whiteboards what they think they have just seen. Ask the children to hold up their whiteboards to show you their words, phrases or sentences.

45. Grammar charades 1

Level: moving on and advanced

GRAMMAR ALERT! Simple sentences – noun verb adjective

✦ In this game one child reads a simple sentence from a card without telling anyone what they have read. The child then mimes this for the class. Can the class guess the mime? Can they write down on their whiteboards the parts of the sentence they have seen for example 'noun verb adjective', rather than the meaning of the mime they think they have just seen? Ask the children to hold up their whiteboards and show you their grammar sentences.

Ask the first child to read the sentence aloud. Can the class match the parts of the sentence to the 'grammar part' sentence they have written?

46. Grammar charades 2

Level: advanced

GRAMMAR ALERT! Sentence construction – noun adjective verb adverb

- In this game one child reads a 'grammar parts' sentence from a card without telling anyone what they have read. The sentences should be made up of grammatical terms such as noun, verb, adjective, adverb rather than words in the target language.

- The children must now think of a sensible sentence in the target language to match the grammatical terms in their 'grammar parts' sentence. For example, if the card says 'noun adjective verb adverb', they must think of a sentence they can mime that has these components in that order, eg

noun	adjective	verb	adverb
le chat	noir	mange	lentement

- The child then mimes this for the class. Can the class guess the mime? Can they write down on their whiteboards the sentence they have seen?

- Ask the children to hold up their whiteboards and show their sentences. Ask the first child to read aloud the 'grammar parts' sentence. Can the class match the parts of the sentence to what they have written?

47. Colour mimes and word association

Level: beginners

✦ Select the colours you want to practise with the children and the new colours you want to introduce. Think of key objects you associate with the colours, for example:

yellow	sun
blue	sea
green	long grass
red	fire
black	dark/eyes shut
white	cold snowball
pink	flower
lilac	butterfly

✦ Create a mime to represent each colour and share these with the children, saying the colour in the target language at the same time.

✦ When you have mimed all the colours, ask the children with a partner to recall as many of the colours as they can in the target language and to decide what each mime represents. Ask one pair to share their ideas with another pair. Take class feedback.

✦ Call a colour – can the children respond with the correct mime? Invite a child to take your place, calling out colours. Can the class respond with the correct mimes?

✦ Ask the children to create mimes of their own for three colours and then to challenge a partner to name the correct colours.

48. Making colour mime messages

Level: beginners and moving on

- Revisit activity 47. Can the class help you place pictures of the objects you mimed next to the correct written colour?
- Mime a colour – can the children write down on a whiteboard the colour they think you associate with the mime?
- Conceal the written word and perform the mime. Can the children recall independently the written word for the colour?
- Can the children solve your physical colour symbol messages? They must observe you creating a physical colour symbol message – a sequence of actions depicting colours and decide which colours are being depicted. They will need to write down the colours as many times as they see you perform the colour symbol and in the correct order.
- Ask children to create their own colour and action spoken message. Can they perform their own colour mime messages for the class?

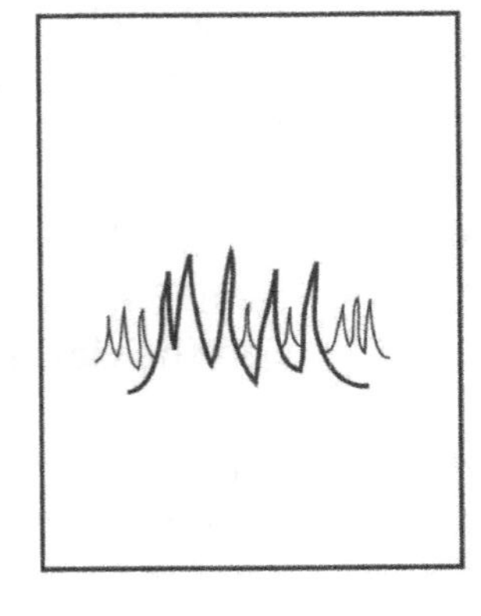

49. Smoke signals

Level: all (can be played at word, phrase, sentence and even text level)

✦ Select four children. Divide them into two pairs and stand the pairs in diagonally opposite corners of the classroom. Give one pair a piece of A4 paper with an empty thought bubble drawn on it. Give the other pair a word, phrase or sentence in the target language. The other children in the class need rough paper and a pencil. The pair with the target language sentence must decide upon how they are going to mime/ act out their information so that the pair in the opposite corner can write down in the empty bubble what they think has been sent, like a smoke signal, to them by the first pair.

✦ The other children in the classroom must also write down in the target language what they think the message sent was.

✦ Ask the pair with the filled-in bubble to share what they have written and ask the class to reveal what they have written. How clear was the smoke signal? Ask the first pair to read out the target language phrase they have tried to act out.

✦ Swap the four children for another four children in the class and set up the challenge a second time .

50. Word shapes

Level: all (particularly good for young learners to internalise the spelling of key target language)

✦ When you write a word it has a shape all of its own. Ask the children to write a list of key words from your current unit of work. Can they now work in groups of six to create the physical sculptures of target language words? Can other children in the class recognise which word they have recreated?

51. Timed word shapes

Level: beginners and moving on

✦ This activity follows on from activity 50. Share a list of key words with the children. Divide the children into groups of six. Tell them that you will say one of the words on the list and they will have 60 seconds to create the word shape. Play the game a second time.

✦ When you play the game a third or fourth time, conceal the written words and only reveal them after the children have formed their word shapes.

52. Word shape galleries

Level: moving on

✦ Ask the children to form their favourite physical word shape and take pictures of these shapes. Create a word shape gallery as a display with the written words around the outside of the photos displayed in a random order. Can the children match the words and the physical word shape photos?

53. Shape, picture and sound sentences

Level: moving on and advanced

- Divide the class into groups of four. You will need cards with different target language sentences on them, one for each group. The sentences should describe an item or an object in the target language; for example if you have been working on food: 'the apples are red and sweet' or 'the sweets are on top of the table'.
- Give each group a sentence. Can the children, working in their groups, create a visual performance of the message using actions, mimes and sound effects?
- At the end of their sentence performances, can the class select the sentence that the children have performed?

54. Shape, picture and sound sentences on film!

Level: moving on and advanced

- This activity continues on from activity 53.
- Can the children, in their groups, write a series of sentences of their own and create shape picture and sound sentence performances?
- Film the performances and let the children record their voices as 'voice overs' to the performance and add their written target language sentences as subtitles.

55. Punctuation personality poses

Level: all (can be played at word, phrase, sentence and even text level)

GRAMMAR ALERT! Punctuation

- With your class, discuss the role that simple punctuation plays in a sentence. If punctuation marks had personalities, what type of personality do they think each item of punctuation might have?

- A question mark is inquisitive. Ask the children to take an inquisitive pose, eg a querying face, tilted slightly to the side, with a finger to the side of the face.

- A capital letter is proud and strong announcing the start of the sentence or, in German, a noun! Ask the children to take the pose with hands on hips and legs slightly apart, standing very upright with a proud face.

- A comma is a pause and a space. Ask the children to take the pose and stand upright with hands spread open in front of them and their faces waiting for a response.

- An exclamation mark wants to be heard! Ask the children to take the pose of someone with a hand in the air attracting attention and wide open eyes, and a grimaced smile as if they really want to be heard.

- A full stop won't let you pass! Ask the children to take the pose of a strong, firm person with one hand on a hip and the other arm stretched out, with the hand in a stop position. Their faces are strong, firm and non-moving, not even a twitch!

- Give each child a punctuation card, with one of the above punctuation marks on it. They must walk around the room and when you say stop, they must show the person nearest them their card. Can that person strike the correct pose for the punctuation mark?

- They swap cards and move on.

56. Punctuation personality pose freeze frame game

Level: all (can be played at word, phrase, sentence and even text level)

GRAMMAR ALERT! Punctuation

✦ This activity follows on from activity 55. Teach the children the names of punctuation in the target language. Ask the children to walk around the room and listen for you to call out a type of punctuation. They must freeze frame and hold the punctuation pose for ten counts. If they move, then they must sit out the next round.

57. Punctuation personality pose pictures

Level: all (can be played at word, phrase, sentence and even text level)

GRAMMAR ALERT! Target language punctuation

✦ Start by revisiting activities 55 and 56.

✦ Discuss with your class the additional punctuation they have seen and are aware of in the written target language. For example:

- Upside down question marks and exclamation marks in Spanish
- Different shaped and positioned speech marks
- Capital letters for nouns in German
- Umlauts in German
- Circumflexes and cedillas in French
- Use of stress accents over vowels in Spanish
- Accents in French.

- Discuss with the children what type of personalities they think these punctuation marks etc have, eg cedillas are soft, quiet and timid whereas upside down question marks want to push their way in first and ask a question.

- Ask the children to investigate poses for the target language punctuation you discuss. During their drama investigations, take pauses and watch what children create.

- Using a large piece of card, cut out a picture frame and take photos of the children in different target language punctuation personality poses. Create a class gallery of punctuation in the target language. The children could create a written background to their pictures made up of words and phrases that demonstrate or contain the punctuation in their picture frame photos.

58. Running commentaries

Level: moving on and advanced

GRAMMAR ALERT! Sentence structure in the target language

- ✦ Children should work in groups of four and create at least four sentences per group.

- ✦ This activity will work best if you revisit the punctuation personality pose activities first (activities 55–57). Ask the children to write several sentences (either supported by a word list and writing frame or as free writing) relating to your current unit of work. Ask them to include a question and a sentence with an exclamation mark.

- ✦ With more advanced learners, ask them to check for any special target language punctuation too. In Spanish, encourage them to try to include a word with stress accents; in French a word with a cedilla or a grave accent over an 'e'. In German remind them to write nouns with capital letters and encourage them to include words with umlauts.

- ✦ They must now attempt to perform their sentences in both a spoken and physical performance. The spoken performance must convey the meaning of the sentences and they must consider voice and attitude as they speak.

- ✦ The physical performance must be a commentary on both the punctuation and the meaning of the sentence. The group will need to decide who speaks; if there are questions and answers, are there two speakers? They also need a person to perform the punctuation poses at the same time, as a running commentary on each sentence, and a person to mime and convey the meaning of each sentence.

- ✦ Practise and then share with the class. You could film these performances and add subtitles too.

59. Movement mobiles

Level: advanced

✦ Divide your class into groups of four. Give each group a written description, which gives them commands and directions to carry out. These directions and commands should generate a movement mobile in the style of an animal or person.

✦ The activity works well with pets, jungle animals, members of the family, characters from a traditional tale like the wolf and the three little pigs etc. Here is a generic example of a written instruction: 'In the style of a grandma, move to the left three steps, turn right slowly, jump up quickly, skip three times.' Ask for volunteers from the group to read out the instructions they have followed and then the group should perform their movement mobile for the class.

60. Message interpreters

Level: moving on and advanced

✦ Working in pairs, children should write a target language sentence or series of sentences based upon the language focus you are covering.

✦ One of the children should read the text aloud that they have written and the second child should act as the physical interpreter of the message.

✦ Swap roles. You could hold class 'watch and listen ins' to see how this is progressing.

61. Simple role on the wall

Level: moving on and advanced

- You will need a large picture of a familiar scene, eg a football game, a picnic, a seaside setting, café.
- The teacher writes notes about the picture on sticky notes and asks for volunteers to come up, read the notes and place them on a relevant part of the picture.
- Children could then be invited to come up and select a sticky note to read out aloud and then perform.

62. More challenging role on the wall

Level: moving on and advanced

- Ask the class to look at a large picture of a scene, eg a football game, a picnic, a seaside setting etc. Can they write a phrase about the picture on a sticky note and then come up and stick their note in an appropriate place on the picture? The phrase could be about something that is happening in the picture, the weather or the feelings of someone.
- Ask for volunteers to come to the front and select a sticky note. They must read the note aloud and then take a pose that reflects the message.
- Remove the picture, but leave the notes in place. Can volunteers read the notes, perform the action or description and, with other volunteers, re-create the poster as the children's notes describe it? Bring back the picture – how similar or different is the volunteers' physical depiction of the picture?

63. Move the message around

Level: all (but beginners should be fairly secure in their ability to read and understand the written word)

✦ How many ways can you interpret a message? Write a message on six pieces of card and hand this message out to six children. Ask them to work with a partner to make sure they understand the message. Together they should decide on an emotion and manner in which to say the message (eg happy, sad, angry, etc), Now listen to the same message six times, as each of the children who was given the card reads out their message using their voice to portray a specific emotion.

✦ Ask the children to pass the cards to six other children. These children must now work with a partner and decide how they will act out and say the message using the same emotion that the person who has just passed them the card conveyed when they read out the message.

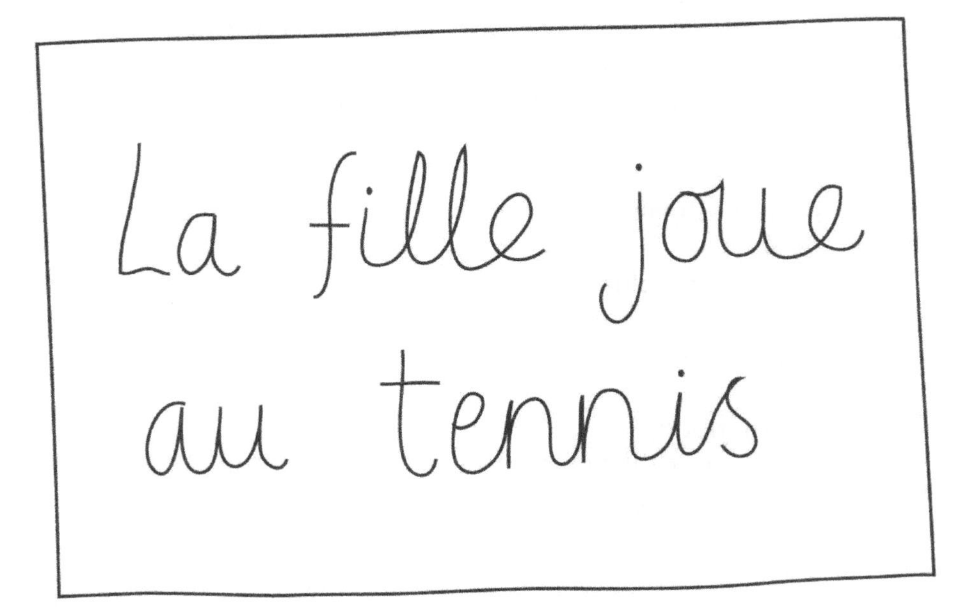

Making a drama out of story and culture!

The activities here allow the children to become creative and generate performances based on stories and cultural events they learn about in their target language lessons. These activities allow the children the opportunity to explore all four skills, as well as grammar and language learning skills of memory and recall.

64. Going on a bear hunt drama!

Level: beginners

✦ In this version of the story 'We're going on a bear hunt' the children make the sounds as they go through the grass, the river, the mud, the wood, the snow storm and finally the cave. For clarity, this activity uses Spanish words/sounds, as an example. All you need to do is replace the sounds with ones more suitable to the target language.

1,2,3
Suish suash, glo glo glorogló
4,5,6
Plochi plochi plop
7,8
Túpiti túpiti tap, suu, uuuu
9,10
Tipi tip tipi tip
¡Ahhhhhhhh! ¡Es un oso!
10,9,8,7,6,5,4,3,2,1

✦ Practise numbers 1–10 first. Set up a path of numbers across the classroom, with the numbers 1–10 repeated three times. The children step carefully across the path of numbers in a line. The children sing / chant the numbers as they walk until the teacher calls stop! The teacher calls out a number and if a child is stood on that number then they are out of the game and caught by the imaginary bear! The teacher can call out more than one number at a time. Ask the children how many bear hunters they think will be left after you have played the game three times.

✦ Once you feel the children know their numbers well enough, ask them to put on their bear hunter kit (imaginary hat, binoculars, wellington boots) and together pretend to go out to see what the terrain is like.

- For each of the terrains (as in the book) there is a sound. Explain to the children that in order to become good explorers, they need to practise the sounds and add actions:

Suish suash glo glo glorogló	river
Plochi plochi plop	mud
Túpiti túpiti tap	forest and owls
Suu, uuuu	snow storm
Tipi tip tipi tip	inside a cave

- Ask the children to close their eyes and come with you on an imaginary journey through the different terrains. The teacher tells the story in English of their journey and the children join in with sounds that 'colour' in the terrain that is described. They are the sound effects.

- Now they are finally ready to become bear explorers! They need to practise the rhyme, remember their actions and their numbers too... but when they get to the end of the rhyme they need to listen for you to shout out / whisper / say very quickly etc, the final line '¡Ahhhhhhhh! ¡Es un oso!'

- When they hear you say the final line, they must freeze frame and stay very still until you have counted backwards very slowly from 10–1. If they move then the bear will catch them!

65. Pop-up posters

Level: moving on and advanced

- Can the children, working in groups of four, take the information from an advertisement (eg for a sports match, a circus or a film) and use it to create a dynamic 3D performance of the information? Each child in the group should be responsible for key information on the poster, eg date, time, cost, venue and activity. They must create a physical and spoken performance of the information and combine this with the performance of the other members of their group.
- Their group performance should be in the style of the poster, eg circus style or football match style.

66. Bringing traditional rhymes and poems up to date in a communal class performance

Level: moving on and advanced

- Share and practise with the children a traditional rhyme, song or poem from the target language.
- Ask the children to suggest ways that, as a communal voice, you can say the rhyme or poem and make it more engaging for a present day audience. Can they add sound effects? Do they need to repeat or stress key words?
- Add a performance element by giving groups within the class the responsibility of adding percussion by clapping, tapping, clicking etc the rhythm of the rhyme or poem. Put together a communal class performance of the traditional rhyme or poem.

67. Let the picture speak!

Level: advanced

✦ Share a picture with the class. It can be a photograph of characters talking in a familiar setting or a picture by a famous artist which has characters talking or taking part in a familiar daily activity.

✦ Brainstorm with your class what target language questions and answers the characters may be saying (using the present tense). Brainstorm also the thoughts that may be running through the heads of the characters depicted (eg about the weather, the food and drink in the picture, what they want to eat and drink, clothes items, what they really think about something someone else is wearing, etc). Record this language on a flip chart or whiteboard clearly visible to all the children.

✦ Divide your class into five working groups. Each group's task is to create a scenario where they write a script, based on target language dialogues from the picture. They must then decide how they will act out what is happening based on the picture. However each group's task will be different. The groups should be asked to consider one specific scenario each:
  - What was happening before the picture is taken?
  - What is really happening in the picture they can see?
  - What will happen after the event they can see in the picture?
  - What is happening with a different group of people in the same setting at the same time as the event in the picture?
  - Finally what is the subplot and what are the characters in the picture really thinking about?

- All the scenarios should be created in the present tense. With the picture as a backdrop on your interactive whiteboard or as a large copy, invite the groups to perform their scenarios.

- As a follow up, take the children to a large open space, place the picture on an easel and designate areas around the picture for each scenario and its characters to sit. Ask them to take the pose of the first part of their written scripts. Allow the children to create props too for their performances. Source and play music which fades in and out at the beginning and end of each performance. One performance should follow another with all the other performances in freeze frames until it is their turn to perform.

- Now let the picture speak! Perform your picture speak performance for another class or in an assembly.

68. Who lives here?

Level: all (can be built upon time and time again to create your own mini class soap opera over four years)

- ✦ Give each table responsibility for a house. Provide the children with a photo of the front door with a number on it. (I often take photos of interesting-looking front doors when I am abroad in target language countries.) The children need to source pictures of the people they think live in the house and create a family tree with target language first names and a family surname. (The children could dress up as the inhabitants of the house and create their own photos.)

- ✦ Over the course of time that the project runs, ask the children to create, using the family members as characters, a folder of simple sketches, monologues, dialogues and descriptions which they must practise and perform too.

- ✦ Let the children film themselves and also create photo albums using an App like Pic Collage. The children will build an e-file of video clips of their performances, Pic Collage photos and sound files of conversations where the characters introduce themselves in the first person singular.

- ✦ The characters can take part in simple activities like breakfast time, going out shopping, cooking, talking about favourite subjects at school, their parents, Christmas, Easter, a festival etc.

- ✦ Take time to revisit the 'Who lives here?' project every time you have an interesting familiar everyday situation in your class learning focus, or when the children have further developed their ability to talk about themselves.

GRAMMAR ALERT! Third person singular present tense sentences

✦ As the children progress in their learning, you can encourage them to describe another person in the third person singular or show us around the inside of the house and describe where items are, what they look like and the position of the items etc!

✦ Why not let the people from the different houses meet each other – at the market, at a café or using public transport (appropriate to the target language country)!

69. Words as strings

Level: moving on and advanced

GRAMMAR ALERT! Commands

✦ The children need to know commands for movement before doing this activity, eg:

- Move your right leg/left leg
- Lift up your arm/ head
- Stand up
- Go forwards (slowly)
- Stop
- Turn around
- Sit down.

✦ Children work in pairs with one being a puppet with strings and the other a puppeteer. The puppet partner starts sitting on the floor. The child who is the puppeteer moves the puppet partner with words, as if they are strings. Can they get their partner to stand up, move arms and legs, walk across the room, turn round, walk back and sit down? They should then swap roles.

✦ Extend this activity by adding adverbs and similes, using nouns that change the puppet's character (eg change the puppet from a person to moving like a type of animal).

70. Words as strings to bring a character to life

Level: moving on and advanced

- ✦ This is a pairs activity. Give the children a picture or story as a stimulus. You will need to pick a picture or character in a story for which the children have the language.
- ✦ Ask the children, separately, to focus on one character in the picture or the story and write a sequence of instructions which match the activity the character is participating in. For example, the Hungry Caterpillar is eating food, growing and becomes a butterfly or, in a painting, a character is walking through the countryside, etc.
- ✦ One child is the puppet and the other the puppeteer. The puppeteer should give commands to make their puppet do particular actions.
- ✦ Ask the children to add adverbs to increase the speed or reduce the speed or the noise of the action.

71. Shadow puppet greetings

Level: beginners

✦ Focus on a well-known traditional tale, such as Goldilocks and the Three Bears or the Three Little Pigs. Repetitive story lines and limited characters are great for this. Discuss the story in English to re-familiarise the children with the story line.

✦ Read the story, if possible, in the target language to the children. Create shadow puppets of the main characters and share these with the children. Using the shadow puppets, introduce the main characters in the target language, practising the character names in the target language with the children. Use different voices and attitudes, eg loud and scary or quiet and frightened. Can the children say the characters' names in the target language to a partner and link the shadow puppets to characters in the story?

✦ Create small shadow puppets with the children and allow them to hold these up behind a lit screen or sheet. Children make their puppets come to life and introduce themselves in the target language to the class.

72. Shadow puppet parade

Level: beginners and moving on

- This activity follows on from activity 71.

- Practise greeting the puppets in the target language, asking the puppets their names and how they are feeling (based on how they feel in the traditional story). How do the children think these puppets would feel and sound? Add this to the performances and ask for volunteers to perform with the puppets how they think they would greet the class. Brainstorm simple questions that the children could ask the puppets (name, age, feelings, what they like or do not like). Select several children to come out and hold the shadow puppets and respond to the questions from the class on behalf of the shadow puppets. Encourage the more advanced learners to use more extended feelings, eg I am hungry / scared / angry / frightened etc.

  Now give every child a small shadow puppet and hold a shadow puppet parade, where the children move around the classroom to music with their puppet. Every so often pause the music and put the 'pretend spotlight' on one or two children. Can they say something for their puppet in character, eg name, age, feelings etc? Start the music again and continue the parade.

73. Puppet phrase exchange

Level: moving on

- ✦ This activity follows on well from the Shadow puppet greetings (activity 71) and the Shadow puppet parade (activity 72).

- ✦ Give children their own smaller versions of the puppets and, in groups of four, ask the children to play a game called 'Say a phrase exchange'. The children say a phrase that matches their puppet and each child in the group of four has a turn to speak and share.

- ✦ Then the puppets are exchanged. The children give their puppet to the child to their right and the activity begins again. The only rule is that the next child can not say what the immediately previous child might have said. Once the game is established, encourage the children to add voices for their puppets.

- ✦ Now add a new dimension where one puppeteer speaks and the other puppeteers must say the same phrase but in the voice of the character of their own puppet.

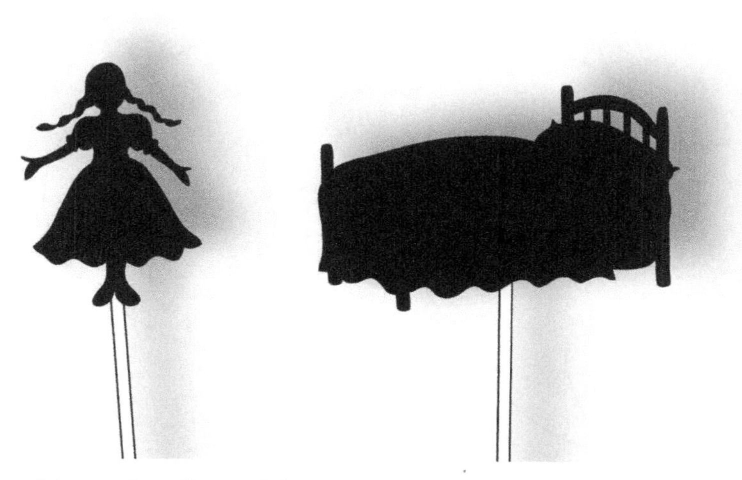

74. 'Who is it?' puppet game

Level: beginners and moving on

✦ In this activity practise introducing puppet characters using a full first person sentence (eg 'Hello I am Goldilocks') or a full third person singular sentence ('Hello, it's Daddy Bear'); they may want to use both types of utterance in their puppet shows. Also allow children to practise the question 'Who is it?'.

✦ Practise the key phrase 'Who is it?' with the children and then ask them to echo your character's voice as they repeat the question after you. Can they decide by the tone of your voice who is asking the question (eg, Dad, Mum, Baby Bear or Goldilocks)? They must respond with a greetings phrase eg 'Hello I am...' or 'Hello it is... '.

✦ Call out a character's name: the children should, after counting 1,2,3, call out the question 'Who is it?'. You should call a character and the children should respond with the key phrase 'Hello I am. + character's name' in the correct tone of voice for that character. This can be played as pairs and in groups to consolidate.

75. Memory props tray

Level: all

- Discuss with the children the items you may need to put on a performance of a traditional story, eg Goldilocks, Red Riding Hood etc (whichever is your class focus). Brainstorm the nouns of the key items that the children may already know and look up unfamiliar items in a bilingual dictionary. (Draw pictures of all the items on a piece of paper to create a 'paper memory tray' (like the memory tray games we have all played in the past). In pairs the children can now play the memory tray mimes game.

- Ask the children to work with a partner and think of mimes and movements that portray the items on the paper memory tray. Suggest that the mimes should portray the object or its use and ask them to add a physical movement that conveys the sound of the word. For example, is it a quick word, a smooth sounding word, a hard quick sounding word etc? (They do not actually say the word but they should mime and move like the word.)

- Join pairs together to create groups of four. Each pair should name the objects and then share their mimes. They can then play a game of memory mime tray, where one pair performs all the mimes but misses out an object. The other pair needs to guess which one it was.

- With developing and moving on learners, ask them to use a key question 'What is it?' and 'What's missing?' and to respond using a full sentence 'It is…' and 'The… is missing.'

76. Colour carnival parade

Level: beginners

- Show the children pictures of carnival masks downloaded from the internet or from books. (These need to be in colour.) Ask children to come out and identify in the target language a colour or colours they can see in the mask. Ask the other children to repeat the colours. Which masks do they like and why?

- Look at a picture of a carnival parade. Ask the children to describe when they have seen people dancing in a parade. What type of movements do they make and what is the rhythm of the music like?

- Hold up strips of different coloured card. Say the colour and demonstrate a physical action to go with that colour. Ask the children to stand up and to try to recall and perform the physical action you demonstrated for each colour. For example:

red	jump
blue	hop twice
green	stretch
yellow	run
black	turn around

- Call out three colours and ask the children to remember the actions and do the actions for the colours in the correct sequence.

- In pairs, ask the children to create actions for six colours. The pairs demonstrate their actions and colours to another pair. Each pair can then challenge the watching pair to perform in sequence the six colours that have just been demonstrated to them.

✦ Create a colour and movement chain. Ask the children in groups of four or five to create colour and movement chains. They can decide whether one child in their group or all the group calls a colour and does/do the associated action. They should, however, use all the colours and perform all the actions.

✦ Ask the groups to now consider rhythm, repetition of the colours, speed, volume and ask them to work as a group to create a dynamic colour and movement chain.

✦ Ask each group to practise their performance and to consider how they could add additional language such as numbers and the action commands.

✦ Ask each group of children to perform their carnival colour movement chains for the class.

✦ Discuss with the class the requirements of a parade:
- Music
- Rhythm
- Colour
- Dynamic action
- A long line of performances passing through a space.

✦ Create a class parade of the different groups colour and movement chains. You could add samba music in between performances that all the children dance to.

Explorations of art and music

The activities here allow the children to become creative and generate performances in their target language lessons using art and music as stimulus and performance tools. These activities allow the children the opportunity to explore all four skills, as well as grammar and language learning skills of memory, recall and creativity with familiar and unfamiliar language.

77. Conveying emotions through art and mirror mime drama

Level: moving on and advanced

- ✦ In this activity children assume the character of people in famous pieces of art. They explore how they might look if they were angry, sad, happy, bored, friendly etc. This adds an exciting and creative dimension! Indeed how might they express this emotion and why?

- ✦ Practise emotions in the target language (which you will later be joining with spoken sentences about likes, dislikes, food, daily activities, places and events). Select up to eight emotions that you want the children to explore with the characters in the pieces of art you give them. The paintings do not need to express these emotions – it's about the children exploring how to convey these emotions and then performing them in the persona of the character they have observed in the painting.

- Share the emotions as facial expressions and word cards with the children. Can they identify the emotion? Is it an emotion that is easy to recognise through the written word or do they need to use visual clues? Take feedback. Give out mirrors if possible and ask the children to say the emotion in the target language and create the facial expression. Can they move seamlessly from one emotion to another? Ask them to watch what changes in their faces to portray the new emotion.
- Practise the emotions in full sentences with the children in the target language, eg 'I am friendly because I am happy'.

- Put the children in pairs in a space where they can stand and face each other. Develop a mirror mime activity. One partner is A and the other partner is B. You, as the artist, tell all the partner A children the facial expression with which they should start the activity. Simply say in the first or third person singular (example here is first person singular) one of the emotions you have introduced eg 'I am happy!' and the children who are partner A should create that facial expression. Partner B must mirror exactly partner A and their facial expression.

- You, as the teacher, must now select another emotion and say 'but now I am angry!'. This is where the mirror mime takes place. Partner B must observe Partner A and as partner A works out how to slowly change their expression from happy to angry; partner B must copy Partner A exactly.

- Swap roles so that Partner B now leads. Complete the activity above a second time.

- Now ask the children to reverse roles again. Announce a new emotion 'I am…'. Partner A creates this facial expression and Partner B must copy. Now, as the teacher, say a new emotion and this time, Partner A must say the statement they hear you say and use a voice that is appropriate to the emotion, while continuing to move from one facial expression to the next. Partner B must copy the voice, the facial expression development and then as you say your next statement, Partner B takes over the lead role and it flows from one partner to the next.

- Ask the children to explore independently, working in their pairs, at least six of the emotions that you have introduced and practised. Hold freeze frames and 'view ins' – where you stop the class and all the class observes work of a pair – then the pairs return to their independent work until you freeze frame again.

78. Six-sided emotions

Level: advanced

- This activity follows on from activity 77. Bring the class back to their tables. Give each table or group (no more than six children) a different portrait to work with, possibly by different artists. The table should decide which six emotions they want to explore with the character in the picture. Each child must create an emotion statement eg 'I am sad' – and think of the voice and the action for the character and share this with their group.

- The group or table must put together their work as a piece of art – a six-sided piece of art (if there are six children in the group). The children will need to decide how they want to stand, sit, perform so that the audience understands that each emotion is a different emotion of the same character. For example, a group of six could stand facing outwards in a hexagon; the hexagon could move round to the right each time a new child performs their emotion – a bit like a carousel. Or some children might like to see their character as something that grows out from the sides of the original piece of art. Each child and its face appears from either side of the child who starts the performance. How many creative performance possibilities can the children create?

- And, finally, ask the children to extend their performances. They need to repeat their six-sided performances but now add, as an aside, a reason why they feel like they do and actions to portray what they are doing.

- Ask the children to show the class their portrait from which they have developed their ideas and to perform their character's six-sided emotions and reasons for their emotions for the rest of the class.

79. Poster power performance poems

Level: advanced

GRAMMAR ALERT! Nouns, verbs, adjectives, adverbs, prepositions

✦ The objective of this activity is to create a class performance poem that shares the flavour and the events of a festival or event in the target language country. First select your event and look carefully at a poster advertising it. You will need to identify and select themes in the poster that you have already practised with your pupils. The children must be able to create full sentences – noun, verb, adjective or adverb – to describe what they see and feel in the poster, for example, the weather / the setting or landscape / the people / the clothes / the feelings and emotions / the food etc.

✦ As a class you need to look at the whole picture and information on the poster. The class needs to help you to brainstorm and source, via dictionaries etc, the language required to describe what they can see, or to bring to life conversations between characters they can see on the poster. You need to gather the language for the Poster power poems performances on a flip chart or whiteboard for reference.

✦ Look carefully at the poster with your class and brainstorm the key target language they can think of to describe what they can see. Identify four main themes that you can see in the poster or picture with your class. Section off the picture and allocate a title to each area, eg weather, clothes, food, people. Record these on a flip chart or a whiteboard, divided into four sections as in the poster above. Record the language the children think of in the correct area.

✦ Working as differentiated ability groups, allocate one focus area to each group in the class. Ask each group to work as a team to create a sequence of sentences – one per child in the group – to describe what they can see. Give the group a formula to work with: noun / verb / adjective or adverb.

- ✦ Now create 'Poster poem performance' sentences.
- ✦ Working in their groups, ask the children to check that they have used the three components in their sentences (noun, verb, adjective or adverb). Can they now order the sentences they have created so that they create a powerful description of their part of the picture? Each child should select a sentence to which they need to add actions and voice (eg calm, fast, powerful, cheering, loud, mechanical, tired). You may at this point want to bring the class back together to explore this idea with a sample sentence from each group or a sentence that you have created. Each group must now order their sentences into a verse of the class poem.
- ✦ It's time now to generate the 'Poster power performance'. Make sure all the children can see the original poster. Ask them, in the style of the poster, to add rhythm and beat to their poem verses that they have created. Each child is responsible for adding this agreed rhythm and beat to his/her sentence. Now your class can perform their poem together as one whole poem about the event as a Poster power performance grand finale!

- ✦ Record each group's poem and performance. Play the performances to the class in a sequence agreed and organised by the class.

80. Linking parts of the body and movements with mime, performance, art and dance

Level: all

✦ To deliver this learning activity you need to source works of art that are based upon the movement of the body, for example, Icarus by Henri Matisse (which is used as an example here).

✦ First teach or revisit the nouns for parts of the body in both singular and plural forms. You could use Robots (activity 18) or Movement mobiles (activity 59) or sing a well-loved song such as 'Heads, shoulders, knees and toes' in the target language. All these activities will get the children up, moving, listening, responding and joining in and thinking about how we move our bodies and how we isolate movement.

✦ Introduce and practise the key instructional language in the target language for:

run	jump	touch
clap	hop	move
walk	crawl	slide
kick	push	

✦ Link the language with an action, create mime performances of the language and the actions. Ask the children to do their actions slowly, quickly, softly etc.

✦ Now call out a part of the body and the class should respond with an action representing the command they think best fits with that part of the body, eg 'hands' – children might respond by clapping or 'legs' children might respond by walking or running... but if you shout 'leg' then maybe they will respond with 'hopping' – as it's on one leg!

- Play the game a second time but this time the children should say the command and do the actions.

- Can the children, working in groups of four, create a flowing movement from one side of the hall to the other which involves them saying a part of the body, then an action, then a part of the body, then another action using the instructional language you have practised with the class? They should use at least five movements and five body parts to get from one side of the room to the other!

- You can change the focus slightly and add challenge by asking the children to call a number of the body parts, eg three legs – so the children will have to demonstrate three people hopping or two children – one running and one hopping.

- If you have iPads, children can take photos or a video of their sequences; back in class they can add their own written statements or record themselves saying the sequence of movements and body parts in time with the video clip or photo show.

- Now start to bring art to life! Using the picture of Icarus, explain that mythical character Icarus wanted to fly but he flew too near to the sun! Can the children make the painting of Icarus move, using appropriate target language and movement? Can the children make Icarus move like he is flying?

- Ask the children to observe the picture of Icarus and make their own performance painting of Icarus by Matisse. They need to paint the body as words and add movements and sound to generate the idea of flying.

81. Weather vanes

Level: all

- Using famous art or music, ask the children to work with a partner to create a physical weather vane using the weather phrases that they know. Weather vanes turn depending on the wind so the pair must interlock arms and move together as one to portray different types of weather and say the weather phrases in a style that depicts the type of weather they are describing.

82. Sport as art and performance

Level: moving on and advanced

- Give the class pictures or posters of sportsmen and women in action. (You could focus on one single sporting event such as the marathon, the World Cup or the Olympics.)

- In pairs, ask the children to create a sequence of three movements that the sports star makes when they move in their specific sport (eg push, run, stop). Can they create a repetitive spoken and mime routine to convey the sport? Ask the pairs to demonstrate to the class their repetitive spoken mime. Now the children should create some percussion background to their performance using their own bodies – hands to clap, feet to stamp, fingers to tap, voices and sounds etc. It should reflect the rhythmical nature of the sporting activity. Can they add this to their performance? This is now a repetitive, rhythmical spoken performance delivered to demonstrate the physical process taking place.

- In a large space or at the front of the classroom, select six performances to be joined together, performing firstly one at a time and then all at the same time to create a physical mime – spoken and percussion performance of the sports chosen.

83. 3D art – bringing characters to life

Level: beginners

GRAMMAR ALERT! First person singular present tense sentences

- I call this activity '3D art' because it involves taking a piece of art and imagining and bringing the characters to life through performance and the use of simple target language. It can be used at different stages of target language learning.
- Here we are considering 3D art as a way to explore present verbs and reinforce personal information about ourselves, eg I am called / I live in / I am...years old / I feel happy, OK, not so good.
- Select a piece of art that has conversation and interaction running throughout the story line of the picture. Make sure there are enough characters for a group of six children to be able to select characters that they want to investigate. One of my favourites is the 'Luncheon of the Boating Party' by Renoir. Set the scene by investigating, as a class, possible phrases in the target language that characters could be saying.
- Practise voices that the characters might have. Add actions to the characters and ask the children to think of signature actions for the characters.
- Divide your class into mixed ability groups of six children maximum and make sure in each group you have a strong linguist and strong performers.
- As you progress through the stages described below, increase the amount of reference sources the children can use, so they can access powerful verbs and adjectives etc.

- Children work in their mixed ability groups of five or six. Each group will need to have a space away from their tables or in the hall and have access to an A3 size colour picture of the painting.
- Each child picks a character in the painting they think looks interesting and thinks of a name for their character. (Children should have had prior experience looking at male and female names in the target language.)
- The children must work out either individually, or with a talking partner, how to say their name, where they live, how old they are and how they are feeling. (You can make this a differentiated outcome task by allowing children the flexibility to decide how much they feel confident to say in the target language – all the statements or just some of them.)
- Now they may like to find a prop, eg a hat / a cup / a glass / a toy pet etc and they must practise their poses so that they look just like they are in the painting itself.
- Each child needs to consider the voice of the character by looking at the pose of the character in the picture and their expression etc.
- Each child in turn performs for a partner and then for their working group their characterisation of the character they have selected, with the chosen actions they have given their character and the phrases in the target language.
- The children now get into pose and create their version of the painting physically. Each character talks in turn from the left to the right of the picture.
- Now it's time to show the class. The groups sit around the room and one by one the groups stand, get into position for their painting and freeze frame exactly like the painting.

- The teacher takes the role of the artist and flicks an imaginary paint brush at each child individually and the characters one by one come to life and perform in the target language.

- The teacher flicks the imaginary paint brush a second time and this time the children freeze frame with their favourite action they have created for their character.

- The next part of the activity is to bring the picture to life in the round. This means when the teacher flicks their hand or brush again, she/he points at a performer in the painting and they start to say their phrases and do their chosen favourite action over and over again until all the characters in the painting are speaking and moving. We are now in the round and the teacher can pause characters or start them up again!

84. 3D art and a virtual gallery – bringing conversations to life

Level: beginners and moving on

GRAMMAR ALERT! Questions and answers – first and second person singular present tense; question words

- You will need three or maybe even four lessons to complete this activity properly. I like to revisit the same picture used in activity 83. This enables pupils, as they progress in their language learning and confidence, to see how much more they are capable of achieving. It also builds a soap opera based on the characters we are getting to know in the picture.

- Children need to be in groups of four or six as every child needs a partner for these activities. You may need to mix up and change who is in each group.

- Revisit the painting and ask the children to remember who they were last time. Can they remember the character they created? If you took photos, take a look through them – perhaps sharing them on the Interactive whiteboard (IWB) so they are more visible.

- The activity this time is for the children to develop conversations in pairs between two characters in the picture. They can recreate their characters and do not necessarily have to use the same personal information as last time.

- As last time, the children need to take the pose of one of the characters, use props to support their characterisation and create their painting as if they are in a picture frame. Now they need to look around their painting and see who it is their character is most likely to hold a conversation with. I encourage the children to let the artist guide them – where is the character and in which direction is the character looking?

- In pairs, the children are to create their conversations. They can use rough paper to make notes if they need to and they should use as many questions and answers as they can (depending on their prior learning).

- The pairs must step back into the picture frame and find a way to walk toward each other, greet each other – all as if they are in the painting – so they may have to walk around an imaginary table that they can see in the painting or get up from a chair etc.

- Working in partnership and remembering to keep in character (through voice, actions, props), the pairs should develop their conversations and work out how to support each other to remember the conversation in the appropriate order and act out their characterisations at the same time! This is not just question answer, question answer etc. It needs to be dramatic and dynamic!

- Once the teacher feels the class is ready to perform, the teacher organises the children in their seats and the first group should come to the front of the class. This is the 'picture frame area' in your virtual gallery classroom now. Even better, display the picture on your IWB and a picture frame too! With an imaginary computer mouse the teacher will hover over a person and that person in the painting must move to meet their partner and start up their conversation. The class listens and watches the animated conversation of the two characters. The teacher will do this three times if there are three partnerships in the painting.

- Swap groups and repeat with a new group.

- You may like to film the groups and then play it back on the IWB at a later date for the class.

- Give each partnership a piece of plain paper and ask them to either draw a still life of the two characters in conversation or a cartoon of the two characters in conversation.

- The children should write out their conversation (using first and second person singular present tense questions and answers) and attach this to the picture they have drawn of their characters.

- Scan the pictures and record the children speaking their conversations and now you have your own virtual gallery – where you can look at a picture and hear the sound file bring characters from the picture to life!

85. 3D art and a whispering gallery

Level: advanced

GRAMMAR ALERT! First, second and third person present tense commonly used verbs to describe people

✦ Revisit the painting you may have used previously to explore 3D art with the children (activities 83–84). If you have the outcomes to hand, ie the virtual gallery of pictures of characters and their conversations, share these with the children.

✦ Now working at their tables in mixed ability groups (with children who work better with support working with either yourself or a partner), give the painting out a third time to the groups. Give each child at the table a cut-out of the face of the character you would like them to be.

✦ They should glue the character to the centre of an A4 piece of paper and write first person singular statements in the target language about the character, based on prompts written by you on a flip chart. Some children may need a writing frame. Prompts could be name, age, where they live, birthdays, feelings, likes, dislikes, what they are wearing, what they are doing. Differentiate the task by outcome – each child must come up with at least five statements for example.

✦ Bring three children to the front to be in the 'hot seat' (prepared to answer questions about their characters using their prepared answers from the A4 sheets they have created) and ask for volunteers in the class to be the question panel. Give these children questions that they will ask the characters at the front, using second person singular questions the class are familiar with, eg what are you called?, what are you wearing? etc.

- The children sitting in the hot seats try to answer as independently as possible and in a voice and with actions that they think suit the characters they have created. (They can use the notes they have written on their A4 sheets.)

- After all three children have been in the hot seat, ask the class to help you to put their statements into a hot seat report on the flip chart. This means that, working with you, they will put the statements into the third person singular using he/she depending on whether the character is male or female.

- Back at their tables, can the groups create appropriate questions in the third person singular, using the hot seat reports and prompts on the flip chart for support? The groups need to think about what the original second person singular question must have been, so that they can try to convert it to a third person singular question.

- Ask the class for suggestions for third person questions to each third person response in the hot seat report. Write these questions up at the bottom of the third person report on the flip chart.

- In groups of four or six, the children become the characters in the painting again (taking poses, thinking of the characters' voices and actions, finding a partner to talk with) but this time the partners will develop a third person singular conversation about one of the other characters in the painting.

- The groups must develop their conversations, work on their characterisation and then hold whispering gallery third person singular conversations to share information about other characters in the painting. Perform these whispering gallery conversations to the class in the picture frame area at the front of the classroom, as described in activity 84.

86. Physical flags

Level: beginners

- This activity practises or revisits and extends colours as the children perform a simple chant and learn names of countries. Children investigate target language flags and create their own target team colour chants.

- Brainstorm the colours that your class have already learned. Introduce flags of different countries. Make sure that the class practises all the colours in the countries' flags that you have chosen.

- One by one bring up on the IWB pictures of country flags (that the children may have seen, for example, in football matches). Show them the names of the possible countries that the flag could represent on the IWB. (If you don't have access to an IWB, you can just print out on card colour pictures of flags and card labels for each country name.) Can any of the children tell you the English name of the country because they recognise the flag? Can the children tell you the colours that are in the flag in the target language?

- Hide the flags on the IWB (or turn over the card versions). Show a country name label. Who can say the colours in the flag?

- Practise actions for each colour, eg blue = sea or rain, red= fire, yellow = sunshine, etc (see activity 47). Ask the children to think of their own actions for the colours. Give children in groups of three or four a flag and the correct name of the country in the target language.

- Can the children make flags that flutter in the wind in a 'Flag Bearer's Ceremony'? Ask the children to create a visual and sound performance of the flag. Working as a team, they must use actions to show what colours are on the flag, and their relative position on the flag (eg are the colours vertical or horizontal stripes?). The group's performance should portray, through mimes and actions, the colours, design and pattern of the flag, as well as the fluttering movement of the flag.

- Use the target language flag as an example for the class. For example the blue, white, red of the French flag could be a vertical flag, where one child stands tallest and says over and over again the target language word for 'blue' accompanied by a repetitive action linked to the colour. A second child kneels and says the colour for 'white' with a repetitive action for white and the final child crouches down and says and does repetitively the action and word for 'red' in the target language.

- Once the children have completed their fluttering flags they can perform them for the class and announce the name of the country in the target language.

87. Au carnaval des animaux – music to inspire performance

Level: all

- Which animals are going to the carnival party? Explain that music can inspire ideas and sometimes composers portray characters through music. In this instance Camille Saint-Saëns has portrayed animals through music.

- Play the children a short excerpt of the music of 'Au carnaval des animaux' to set the scene and ask the children to think of the animals they can hear in the beat / rhythm of the music.

- Explain that the animals are going to the carnival. Introduce the names of animals that may be at the carnival in the target language. Do the children think that any of these animals are depicted in the music?

- Tell the children that all the animals want to go to the party. The animals are loud and lively. They all want to talk and chatter at the same time!

- Can the children help you to create actions to link to the syllables in their target language names?

- Practise the names of the animals, using physical phonics techniques for the sounds of the names.

- Can the children help you to create actions and sounds to represent each of the animals?

- It's the class' responsibility to get the animals and their nouns and actions to the party. Ask the children to pick their favourite animal, then perform the relevant actions and sounds for their partner. Pairs then share their favourite animals with a second pair.

- Play the music quietly in the background and ask the children to go to the party as the animals – walking round the room, sharing their sounds and actions. They should listen to each other, observe each other's actions and then swap animal actions and sounds, then move on to another person with their new animal actions and sounds. If you pause the music they must freeze frame as the animal with one of its actions. Start the music again.

- At the end of the activity – how many of each animal can you find in the room? Call an animal name and, as a class, count up in the target language the number of that animal, while the children acting out that animal make their sounds and actions.

- Let's be creative with the musical story! Create a class dance performance or a class parade of the animals going to the carnival party.

88. Creating a potion performance out of a verb

Level: advanced

GRAMMAR ALERT! The verb 'to have'; singular and plural nouns

- ✦ The focus here is on creating a potion using the verb 'to have' and a recipe for a fantastical or magical character.
- ✦ The activities are based around a magic potion rhyme and the children explore the use of a verb in the target language in the present tense through a creative performance.
- ✦ Ask the children to help you to think of items you may like to add to a potion to create a good wizard and to create a bad wizard. Look up the words with the children in a bilingual dictionary and investigate with the children ways we may say the items to portray the smell, touch and feeling of these items.
- ✦ Practise the verb 'to have' in the target language. You should create actions for each of the parts of the verb – as if you all have wizards wands. Possible actions could be:

I have	point to yourself
you have	point to someone else
he has	point to a boy, nod your head at him and wag your finger at a girl
she has	point to a girl, nod your head at her and wag your finger at a boy
we have	make a large gesture with both arms that encircles all
you have (plural)	point to two people
they have	point to half the class and wag a finger at the other half of the class

- ✦ Ask the class to be magician's apprentices and to think about the actions. With a partner they should practise the wizard wand actions for the verb 'to have' and say the parts of the verb.

- ✦ In pairs now ask them to hold a 'magician's apprentice battle'. It's a simple game of challenging each other to do the correct action for a part of the verb 'to have'. Remind the children that they must remain in magical character all the way through the battle as magicians' apprentices! Hold 'listen ins' and watch some of apprentices go to battle! (This means you should watch two children in battle – one child calling a part of the verb and the other child performing the action.)

- ✦ Ask the children in pairs to create a potion for either a good or a bad wizard. The children should use the nouns you brainstormed earlier for good and bad wizards to create a performance of the magic potion. Each noun should be associated with one of the verbal phrases from the verb 'to have' in the target language.

- ✦ How magical can they make their potion performances?

89. Cinderella and a masked ball pantomime

Level: advanced

GRAMMAR ALERT! The verb 'to be'

- Introduce the class to each of the characters in Cinderella and their names in the target language. The children need to either make or source masks to represent each of the main characters in the story.

- Encourage the children to create a voice for each of the characters or groups of characters – to introduce themselves using the phrase 'I am…' Ask, for example, what do they think Cinderella's voice may sound like etc?

- Practise for each of the characters the phrase: 'I am + character name'.

- Do the children know how to introduce both ugly sisters together? Share with the class how you would say 'We are the ugly sisters'. Can the children spot the difference between 'I am' and 'we are'? Put on your ugly sister voices and practise how the ugly sisters would introduce themselves as individuals and as two sisters (I am… / we are…).

- Practise the question 'Who are you?'. Play a game of Quiz quiz swap: each child has a small version of the picture of either one character or the two ugly sisters which they must show a partner when asked in the target language 'Who are you?' Children must answer either 'I am…' or 'we are…' with the correct character's name and a voice for their character. After both of the children have asked the question and given a response, they then swap cards and move on to a new partner in the class.

✦ Share with the class the parts of the verb 'to be'. Add actions and create a chain reaction. This means that the class stands in circles made up of groups of six children and must try to say the whole verb with actions and pointing to correct numbers of people or boy(s), girl(s) to create a full verb chain reaction. Watch several performances of verb chain reactions.

✦ Tell the children they are now your actors in a pantomime. Reveal on the flip chart all six parts of the verb 'to be' in the target language used with the names of the Cinderella characters. eg:

- We are the ugly sisters.
- They are the prince and Cinderella.

Working in pairs, can children say the phrases on the flip chart and add emotion and feeling...pantomime style? Hold 'listen ins'!

✦ You will need face masks for each of the characters (on sticks with gaps cut out for eyes). Introduce the face masks and ask for volunteers to select a mask and come to the front and in character introduce themselves as the pantomime character.

✦ Divide the class into groups of six and give each group a die. On each face of the die should be one of the characters from Cinderella.

✦ They roll the die and the first game is to try and collect all the characters. They need to take it in turns to roll the die and they must introduce themselves as the character they see, using the verb 'to be' – pantomime style, of course.

✦ To win this game, they must be the first person in the group to be able to say all the characters names. If they throw a character they have already said, then they must miss a go.

✦ Practise how to ask:
- Who is she?
- Who are they?
- Who are you?
- Who is he?

✦ Practise this as a call and response activity in the style of each of the characters in the story.

✦ Play the die game a second time but this time as a whole class activity. Sit or stand the class in a circle. A child rolls the die and must ask a question relevant to the picture they see about who the person is, eg 'Who is she?' The child can decide to whom they pose the question. The question must be asked pantomime style and responded to pantomime style in the character of the face rolled on the die.

✦ Can the children, working in groups of four or six, create a pantomime masked ball performance of 'Who are you?' based on the Cinderella story and using all four questions and all six possible responses?

Sketches

The suggestions below provide opportunities to develop simple sketches and more complex plays and presentations. These sketches allow the children to combine all four skills and grammar they already have practised in class in entertaining and imaginative performances.

90. Simple start sketches!

Level: all

✦ Take a simple theme or focus and create a dialogue of questions and answers that your children can read in pairs. They can practise the dialogues and perform these for the class.

91. Simple start sketches with a surprise!

Level: all

✦ Take a simple theme or focus and create a dialogue of questions and answers that your children can read in pairs. They can practise the dialogues and perform these. Before they share them with the class, they should add an additional question and answer... just for the element of surprise!

92. Simple start sketches with a surprise to swap!

Level: all

- This activity continues on from activity 91.

- Now match pairs together and ask each pair to observe the performance of the other pair. They must now try to replicate the performance of the first pair exactly. Once the second pair has re-performed the first pair's dialogues with the surprise question and answer, the two pairs swap roles and the activity is repeated.

93. Turn down the sound and create your own sketch

Level: moving on

- Play a simple video clip of a role play based on an everyday event in the target language – role plays from the BBC Language Learning Zone would be really useful here. Let the children watch and listen. Now replay without the sound.

- Ask the children in pairs to create a new conversation based on the role play, that they can later perform as the two people in the film clip. Give the children time to write and practise their sketches before asking for volunteers to perform their 'voice overs' for the sketches, while the film clip plays silently in the background.

94. Making a sketch of a traditional story

Level: moving on

✦ In this activity learners create their own very simple versions of a traditional tale. Goldilocks works well because of the simplicity and repetition of the story. The children should work in groups of four, after having listened to a retelling of the story and, if possible, watched a target language version of the story too. You can decide to give the children writing frames to support them with this or you can encourage them to work from memory and prior knowledge and use bilingual dictionaries for support. Each performance can be shown to a small group of children in KS1 or Year 3.

95. Restaurant sketches go head to head!

Level: moving on

✦ Provide the children with a restaurant scenario. Give the children a menu for a restaurant, a picture of a restaurant and a picture of customers and a waiter or waitress. Explain that half the class will create a positive role play and half the class will create a negative role play about the restaurant and a meal. You will need to divide the class into groups of minimum three people (two customers and a waiter).

✦ Once the children have created their role plays, match a negative group with a positive group and let them act out their sketches for each other back to back.

✦ Ask for volunteers to share their negative and positive experience role plays with the class.

96. A radio sketch

Level: advanced

✦ Give the children a simple sketch for four people with questions and answers in the target language. Ask them to work in groups of four to annotate the sketch (in English) with sound effects and music. Can they practise the sketch in their fours, add character to the roles and combine this with the sound effects and music?

✦ Children can record themselves and the clips can be played back to the class as if from the radio.

97. News report as a performance

Level: advanced

GRAMMAR ALERT! Descriptions in third person singular present tense

✦ Nominate a child in a group of four children to be the news reporter at a cultural event, eg a carnival. Their role is to explain in the third person singular what he/she can see and what there is to do, eat, etc.

✦ The role of the other three children is to be people in the crowd. They will take part in dialogue, or cheer and shout like a crowd, or be interviewed by the news reporter.

98. Tour guides

Level: advanced

- Play a clip or show the children a series of pictures of famous landmarks in a target language city. Familiarise the children with the city and key buildings; revisit prior learning of places in the town and directions (eg on your left, on your right, here we can see...). Practise with different voices.

- Give children five minutes to create their own 10 simple sentences, providing a quick guide to the city. Invite volunteers up to share their city guide with the class, either with a clip of the city in the background or using the pictures of the famous city landmarks that you shared with the class.

99. Apps and sketches

Level: all

- Give the children a simple sketch for two people with questions and answers in the target language. Can they practise the sketch and add character to the roles? Now allow the children to use an App such as Sock Puppets to create their own puppet sketch. They should add their own voices, along with sound effects and music from the App. The clips can be played back to the class as if from the radio.

100. Lights, camera, action

Level: advanced

- Provide the children with play scripts with no stage directions and without named characters for each utterance. The scripts should have a twist or a funny ending. Provide the children with the names of the characters in the play.

- Ask the children, in groups of four, to read the play scripts and decide who says which line. Ask the children to add English stage directions too! This is a really good way of developing the children's reading comprehension as you will be able to see how much of the text they can understand. Do they understand the twist at the end and are they able to allocate characters to the utterances? Now the children need to bring the sketch to life by practising and performing it.

101. Sell it to me!

Level: moving on and advanced

- Give each group of four children an item to sell. If you have been focusing on clothes then this can be an item of clothing; alternatively, if your focus has been food then the children could be trying to sell a meal or food. Ask the children to work in their groups to create a radio advertisement which contains a dialogue, a description and a musical element about the item they are selling. Each group can perform their advertisements for the rest of the class.

102. The ultimate presentation

Level: moving on and advanced

- Set groups a task to create the ultimate presentation which focuses on part of the culture of the target language country, eg the beach, the town, a funfair in the target language country, a special event or festival.

- The children should work in groups of four and should design a simple sketch which includes a dialogue, a description of an event or a place, sound effects, a song or rap that explains why the event is good.

- The children then go head to head against other groups in the class and are given marks for clarity, entertainment value and effectiveness from their class. Which group will have created the 'ultimate presentation'?

103. Do you have the X factor?

Level: all

- Provide pairs of children with the words to a song or rhyme that they have already explored and learned during their language learning in the year. Ask the children to create a performance of the rhyme or song. It can: include props, be spoken as a rap, be sung or performed as a sketch. How will they make their mark on the text and do they have the X Factor? Nominate three children in the class to be the X Factor judges and to mark the performances out of 10. Who will win?

Index

Lightning Source UK Ltd.
Milton Keynes UK
UKOW06f0511050316

269652UK00002B/9/P